Dear Parent:
Your child's love of reading starts here!

Every child learns to read in a different way and at his or her own speed. Some go back and forth between reading levels and read favorite books again and again. Others read through each level in order. You can help your young reader improve and become more confident by encouraging his or her own interests and abilities. From books your child reads with you to the first books he or she reads alone, there are I Can Read Books for every stage of reading:

SHARED READING
Basic language, word repetition, and whimsical illustrations, ideal for sharing with your emergent reader

BEGINNING READING
Short sentences, familiar words, and simple concepts for children eager to read on their own

READING WITH HELP
Engaging stories, longer sentences, and language play for developing readers

READING ALONE
Complex plots, challenging vocabulary, and high-interest topics for the independent reader

ADVANCED READING
Short paragraphs, chapters, and exciting themes for the perfect bridge to chapter books

I Can Read Books have introduced children to the joy of reading since 1957. Featuring award-winning authors and illustrators and a fabulous cast of beloved characters, I Can Read Books set the standard for beginning readers.

A lifetime of discovery begins with the magical words **"I Can Read!"**

Visit www.icanread.com for information
on enriching your child's reading experience.

I Can Read!

BEGINNING
1
READING

Pinkalicious®
and the Cupcake Calamity

For Sophia

—V.K.

The author gratefully acknowledges
the artistic and editorial contributions
of Robert Masheris and Natalie Engel.

I Can Read Book® is a trademark of HarperCollins Publishers.

Pinkalicious and the Cupcake Calamity
Copyright © 2013 by Victoria Kann

PINKALICIOUS and all related logos and characters are trademarks of Victoria Kann. Used with permission.

Based on the HarperCollins book *Pinkalicious* written by
Victoria Kann and Elizabeth Kann, illustrated by Victoria Kann
Printed in the United States Of America.
Library of Congress catalog card number: 2012956496

ISBN 978-0-06-218777-2 (trade bdg.)—ISBN 978-0-06-218776-5 (pbk.)

13 14 15 16 17 LP/WOR 10 9 8 7 6 5 4
❖
First Edition

I Can Read!

BEGINNING
1
READING

Pinkalicious®
and the Cupcake Calamity

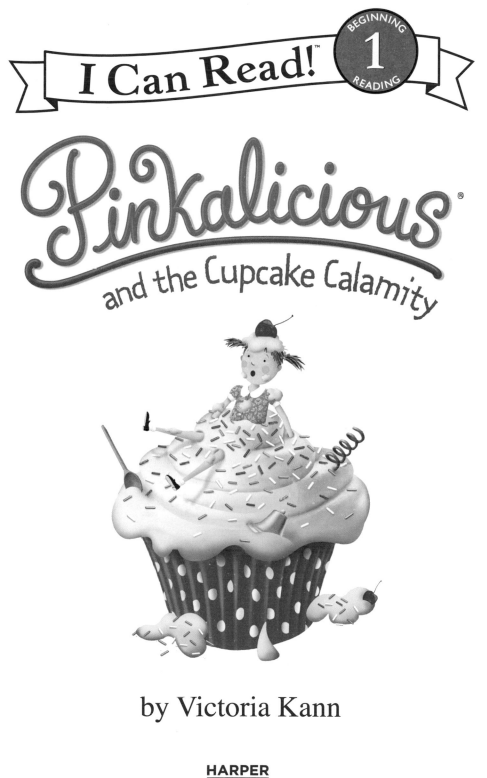

by Victoria Kann

HARPER
An Imprint of HarperCollinsPublishers

One Sunday morning,

we saw a huge crowd outside

Mr. Swizzle's ice cream shop.

I stopped to see what was happening.

"Step right up, folks,"

Mr. Swizzle called.

Behind him was a pink curtain.

"Prepare your taste buds,"
said Mr. Swizzle.
"Dessert is about to be served!"
He lifted the curtain.
The crowd gasped.

Right in front of me was the biggest,

fanciest machine in the world!

Lights were flashing.

Gears were turning.

It hummed, buzzed, and beeped.

"Behold," said Mr. Swizzle,
"my Cupcake-Create-O-Matic!
Just add a dollar and your cupcake
will bake right on the spot!"
I couldn't wait to try it.

BUZZ

HUMM HUMM

BEEP BEEP

Ice Cream

"Me first!" I said.

I ran to the machine

and put in my dollar.

I chose a strawberry cupcake

with pink frosting and pink sprinkles.

I pressed the green button.

Nothing happened.

"Bake!" I said, pressing again.

But no cupcake came out.

"Let me try," said Alison.
One after the other,
people put their money in.
But nothing came out.

"What's going on here?"

The crowd started to grumble.

People were getting upset.

So was I.

I wanted my cupcake!

"I'm so sorry," said Mr. Swizzle.
"Let me get the owner's guide.
I'll have this fixed in a jiffy."

I couldn't wait that long.

I wanted a pink cupcake!

Hmmm . . . I thought.

I looked hard at the machine.

I walked around to the back.

There was a little door

big enough to squeeze through.

So I did!

The Cupcake-Create-O-Matic
was amazing inside!
Mixing bowls whirred
as batter stirred.
Sprinkles and frosting
drizzled everywhere.

I started poking around.

The batter was blending nicely.

It tasted good, too.

There were belts full of
cupcake wrappers,
all ready to be filled.
I swapped out the plain ones
for ones with polka dots.

Then I saw that
only half of the machine
was working.
The mixers weren't pouring batter
into the wrappers.

"There must be a power switch
in here somewhere,"
I said to myself.
I looked up and there it was!

The switch was way up

at the top of the machine.

I climbed all the way there.

"It's cupcake time!" I said

as I flipped it on.

The Cupcake-Create-O-Matic
started rumbling right away.
In fact, it started rattling.
Then, it started shaking.
"Uh-oh," I said.

The machine started filling up
with batter!

"I want to eat a cupcake," I said,

"not BE a cupcake!"

Something was definitely wrong.

The machine shook from side to side.

The walls were starting to crack.

"What is going on?" I cried.

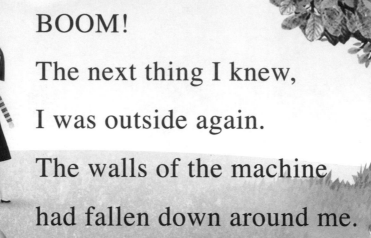

BOOM!

The next thing I knew,

I was outside again.

The walls of the machine

had fallen down around me.

I was sitting on top
of the world's biggest cupcake.

"Pinkalicious!" cried Mr. Swizzle.

"What are you doing up there?

Are you okay?"

I blinked. I smiled.

"Yes. I am perfect!

In fact, I couldn't be better,"

I said.

The crowd roared with laughter.

Mr. Swizzle looked relieved.

"Dig in, everyone!" he said.

Everyone loved the giant treat.

"Sorry about your machine,"
I told Mr. Swizzle.
"That's okay, Pinkalicious," he said.
"From now on, I'll stick to ice cream
and leave the cupcakes to you!"